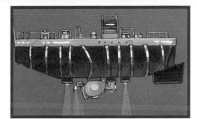

SHIPS *and* SUBMARINES

Written by
IAN GRAHAM

Illustrated by
DAVE ANTRAM

Created and designed by
DAVID SALARIYA

BOOK HOUSE

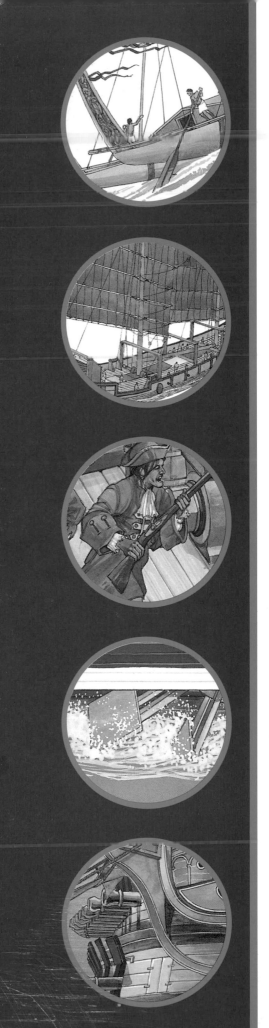

S[S]S and
SU[B]NES

Falkirk Council

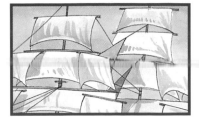

Author:

Ian Graham was born in Belfast, Northern Ireland, in 1953. He studied applied physics at The City University, London, and took a postgraduate diploma in journalism at the same university, specialising in science and technology journalism. After four years as an editor of consumer electronics magazines, he became a freelance author and journalist. Since then, he has written more than one hundred children's non-fiction books and numerous magazine articles.

Artist:

Dave Antram was born in Brighton in 1958. He studied at Eastbourne College of Art and then worked in advertising for 15 years before becoming a full time artist. He has illustrated many children's non-fiction books.

Series creator:

David Salariya was born in Dundee, Scotland, where he studied illustration and printmaking. He has illustrated a wide range of books and has created many new series of books for publishers in the UK and overseas. In 1989 he established The Salariya Book Company. He lives in Brighton with his wife, illustrator Shirley Willis, and their son.

Editors:

Karen Barker Smith
Stephanie Cole

Published in Great Britain in 2002
by Book House, an imprint of
The Salariya Book Company Ltd
25 Marlborough Place, Brighton BN1 1UB

The Salariya
Book Co. Ltd

Visit the Salariya Book Company at:
www.salariya.com
www.book-house.co.uk

ISBN 1 904194 11 7

A catalogue record for this book is available
from the British Library.

Printed and bound in China.

Printed on paper from
sustainable forests.

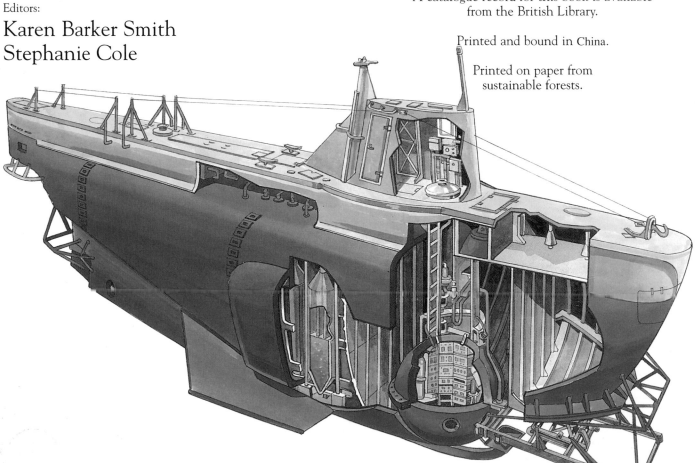

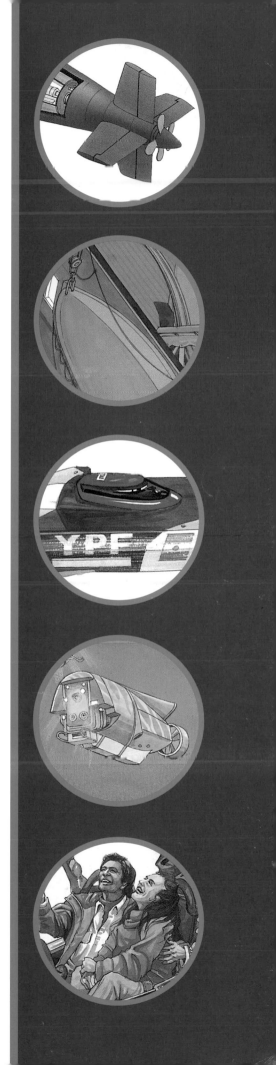

Floating and Paddling

Ancient Egyptian reed boat

Tens of thousands of years ago, long before there were any boats, people had to find ways of crossing stretches of water. The first floating craft were simply treetrunks, or animal skins inflated like balloons. These same materials were later developed into the first boats.

About 20,000 years ago, people had the tools to hollow out treetrunks to make dugout canoes. In places where there were few trees large enough to make dugouts, they covered wooden frames with skins or tree bark to make canoes. Round boats called coracles were made from a frame of woven willow shoots covered with animal skin. In ancient Egypt, people gathered papyrus reeds together to make boats. These reed boats were so light that they could be carried overland easily. Larger boats were made by binding wooden planks together. To push boats through the water, people made broad wooden paddles. A paddle at the back of the boat also helped steer it. As soon as people learned how to build boats, they explored nearby coasts. Boats enabled them to form trading links with other people and sometimes to wage war on them.

About 2,500 years ago, ancient Egyptians built small boats by tying bundles of papyrus reeds together (above). The reeds floated because their stalks were full of air.

People could float out onto rivers on animal skins blown up with air (above). Lashed together, they made simple rafts.

A giant octopus is pictured attacking a sailing ship (left). Sailors returned from long voyages with tales of their adventures. They sometimes claimed to have seen sea monsters like this that could drag a ship beneath the waves, never to be seen again.

The largest Native American canoes were war canoes (above). They could be up to 30 m long with enough room for up to 20 paddlers to sit inside and paddle them through the water. Often they had elaborate designs painted or carved on their sides to give them good luck for battles and to terrify the enemy.

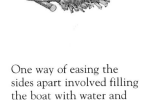

Building a dugout canoe

Building a dugout canoe began with hollowing out a treetrunk. The wood was chopped out using axes and burned out with fire.

Next, the outside of the trunk was carved into a boat shape. Then the sides were eased apart and held with strong wooden struts wedged into place.

One way of easing the sides apart involved filling the boat with water and lighting a fire underneath it. The hot water softened the wood.

Catamaran

Pacific and Indian Ocean islanders made their canoes more stable for use in the open sea (above) by fitting floats called outriggers to them or lashing two canoes together to make a catamaran.

Native American war canoe

Sealskin kayak

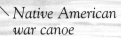

Native Americans used tree bark to build canoes. The shape of the boat was marked on top of the strips of bark with wooden stakes (above).

Next, the bark was pulled into place to form the sides of the boat. More wooden stakes were hammered into the ground to hold it up.

The bark was sewn into position and finally it was stiffened by fitting more wooden struts and curved 'ribs' inside the boat.

In the Arctic, the Inuit people built kayaks: one-man canoes made of frames of driftwood covered with sealskins (above). The skins were sewn together and soaked in water. The wet skins were laid over the frame and as they dried they tightened around it.

7

Oars and Sails

The largest boats and ships prior to the 20th century were propelled by oars or sails. Trading ships relied on sails alone, because there was no room inside their cargo holds for oarsmen. Without such cargoes to carry, warships and grand ships of state had the necessary space for oarsmen. They were put to work to go into battle or when the wind dropped and the sails were of no use. A ship with two rows of oarsmen sitting on each side was called a bireme. A quinquereme ship could hold up to five rows of oarsmen on each side.

Many of the great voyages of discovery and exploration were undertaken in sailing ships. Viking longships carried people to North America 500 years before Christopher Columbus' famous voyages. Columbus was trying to find a new route to the Far East in 1492, unaware that the continent of America was in the way. At about the same time, the Portuguese explorer Vasco da Gama found a route to India by sailing around Africa. In the 18th century, Captain James Cook claimed Australia for Britain while on a scientific voyage to the South Pacific.

Ancient Egyptian cargo ship

In about 2600 BC, the ancient Egyptians built ships (above) to carry cargo up and down the River Nile and also to trade with lands across the Mediterranean Sea.

Greek trireme

A Greek trireme (left) dating from about 600 BC was a formidable warship. It had a total of 170 oarsmen sitting in three rows on each side. Rowed warships were also called galleys.

Viking longship

Roman merchant ship

Roman merchant ships of about AD 100 were steered by two oars at the stern (above left).

Longships (top) carried Viking warriors on raids to northern Europe 1,200 years ago.

Chinese junk

Large seagoing sailing ships called junks (above) were being built in China from about the 13th century.

Santa Maria

In 1620 the Pilgrims set sail across the Atlantic Ocean in the *Mayflower* to escape religious persecution. They landed at Plymouth, in Massachusetts, USA, where they set up the first permanent New England colony.

Columbus' ships *Santa Maria*, *Pinta* and *Niña* discovered the Bahamas and West Indies in 1492. The *Santa Maria* (right) was wrecked on the return voyage and sank.

Mayflower

Endeavour

In 1769, Captain James Cook sailed HMS *Endeavour* from England to Tahiti to observe the planet Venus crossing the face of the sun.

Pirate Attacks

Merchant ships held rich pickings for bands of criminals who roamed the high seas. Phoenician trading ships (from ancient ...hern Syria) fell victim to pirates in the ...iterranean Sea more than 3,000 years ...and pirates still attack merchant ships ..., especially in the Far East.

...racy was at its height in the 17th and ...centuries, especially in the Caribbean ...where trading ships collected rich ...es bound for Europe from the New ... Many countries also secretly ...yed pirate ships called privateers to ...reasure from the ships of other nations. ...cal pirate ship of the day was ...0 m long with up to a dozen guns on ...d carried as many as 150 men. Ships ...hallow hull were favoured because ...ld hide in inlets and rivers where ...litary vessels could not follow them.

When a merchant ship was spotted, the pirate vessel pounded it with its guns to smash the masts and rigging. When the ship was crippled, the pirate vessel came alongside so that the pirates could board it.

...hips flew flags showing symbols of death and ... to terrorise their victims. The most famous ...g was the Jolly Roger – a skull over crossed ...r bones.

Jolly Roger flag

Steamships

The invention of the steam engine by Thomas Newcomen in 1712 led to an industrial revolution on land. More efficient and increasingly powerful steam engines built by engineers like James Watt in the 1760s led to a similar mechanical revolution at sea. The first steamships were built in France and the USA in the 1780s, but they were unsuccessful. Their engines often broke down and they were not powerful enough to do any useful work.

Paddle steamer tug

Many of the earliest paddle steamers were put to work as tugboats. They towed heavy barges and larger ships on rivers and canals and also into and out of harbours.

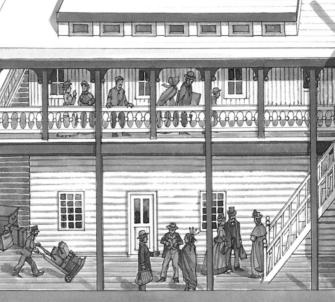

The first practical steamship was the *Charlotte Dundas*. It was built in Scotland in 1802 to tow barges up and down the Clyde Canal. Its steam engine turned a paddlewheel and the broad wooden paddles fixed to the wheel pushed against the water to drive the boat along. Small riverboats often had a single paddlewheel at the stern (back) of the boat, while larger seagoing vessels had two paddlewheels, one on each side of the hull.

Clipper

River paddle steamer

The paddlewheels that drove the early steamships were not ideal. If the ship rolled from side to side in a rough sea, each wheel would rise out of the water alternately. The wheels on the outside of the hull were also easily damaged.

It was the invention of the propeller in the 1830s that ended the age of sail. In 1845 two ships, the _Rattler_ and _Alecto_, had a race and a tug-of-war to find out whether paddlewheels or propellers were the best. The propeller-driven _Rattler_ won both contests, and navies started building steam-powered warships with propellers.

The _Great Eastern_, built in 1858, was 210 m long and could carry 4,000 passengers and 6,000 tonnes of cargo. It failed as a liner because it rolled from side to side too much and was used instead to lay telegraph cables under the Atlantic Ocean.

Great Eastern

The last commercial sailing ships were the clippers (left) that brought cargoes of tea from China to Europe in the 19th century. Their long, narrow hulls were built for speed and their holds were packed full of wooden tea chests.

Special types of paddle steamers (above) carried passengers and cargo up and down American rivers such as the Mississippi, Missouri and Ohio in the 19th century. They had shallow, flat-bottomed hulls, that enabled them to avoid the shifting sandbanks that lay just below the water's surface. The largest of these river vessels weighed over 5,000 tonnes and had up to six passenger decks.

Warships

Warships are more than just fighting ships. They are symbols of a country's power and wealth. If a country can command the seas, it can control trade between countries and add to its own riches. As the powerful European trading nations began to understand this in the 16th century, they built up large fleets of warships.

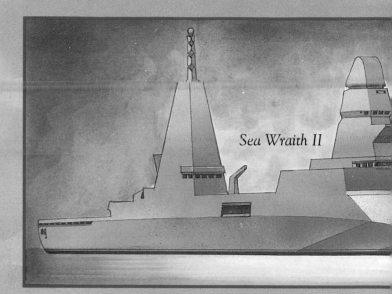

Sea Wraith II

Galleon

A typical English galleon of the time was 43 m long with 38 guns, a crew of 320 sailors and a fighting force of 100 soldiers. Warships like this enabled the English fleet, commanded by Sir Francis Drake, to defeat the Spanish Armada in 1588. Warships roughly doubled in size by the end of the 18th century. By then, building a warship required the wood of 2,000 oak trees.

The hulls of wooden ships were attacked by marine worms. Some ships were protected by covering the underwater part of the hull with lead. Wooden warships usually had a double hull made from oak up to 46 cm thick, with tar-soaked horse hair or rope packed into the space between the two hulls. The tar preserved the wood and discouraged the worms.

The most advanced warship design today is the *Sea Wraith II* stealth ship (left). Its sleek futuristic shape and the latest military technology make it more difficult to spot on an enemy's radar screen. In addition, it can cloak itself in a fine mist of cold water to cool hot spots such as its engine exhausts. Cooling the ship makes it more difficult for heat-seeking missiles to find it. *Sea Wraith II* has not yet been built. Its design is being developed further by the navies who may operate it in the future.

Warship designers play a deadly cat-and-mouse game with weapons designers. Submarines, torpedoes and mines made large battleships obsolete in the early 1900s. Later, missiles replaced heavy guns as the main weapon at sea. Most modern warships are smaller, faster and more manoeuvrable. Only aircraft carriers have continued to increase in size.

Ironclad

During the 19th century, ships' guns became bigger and more powerful, and they fired explosive shells that could smash a wooden hull to pieces. In the 1850s, warships were strengthened to protect them from these terrible weapons by covering their hulls with iron plates 10 to 25 cm thick. This new type of iron-covered wooden warship was called an ironclad.

The *Turtle* (a) was a one-man submarine built to attack enemy ships in 1776. *Nautilus* (b), built in 1800, could raise a sail on the surface. *Argonaut* (c) was a diving bell on wheels that was dragged across the seabed by a diver.

The *Hunley* (d) was the first submarine to sink an enemy vessel, in 1864, but it was also sunk itself! The *Resurgam* (e), built in 1879, was propelled underwater by high-pressure steam.

The Underwater World

Underwater exploration began in the 17th century with the first attempts to build a submarine. A Dutchman, Cornelis Drebbel, is thought to have built the first submarine, which he rowed up the River Thames through London in 1620. It resembled a rowing boat sealed on top with greased leather. More attempts to build submarines in the 19th century produced boats that were slow and difficult to steer. The first practical submarine was built in 1900 by Irishman John Philip Holland. It was powered by a car engine on the surface and an electric motor when submerged. Petrol and diesel engines cannot be used underwater even now because of the poisonous fumes they produce.

Submarines were used in large numbers in both world wars. Sonar, developed during the First World War, enables submarines to detect ships, other submarines and objects near them by bouncing pulses of sound off them. They dive by flooding their ballast tanks with water and surface by blowing the water out again with compressed air. Rudders and tilting fins called hydroplanes control steering. The largest submarines are nuclear-powered vessels that can stay submerged for several months. The smallest are submersibles and bathyscaphes – deep-diving craft used for research and exploration.

Valiant

The British nuclear submarine *Valiant* (above) is 87 m long and displaces about 5,000 tonnes when fully submerged. It is operated by a crew of 103 officers and men.

Second World War submarine

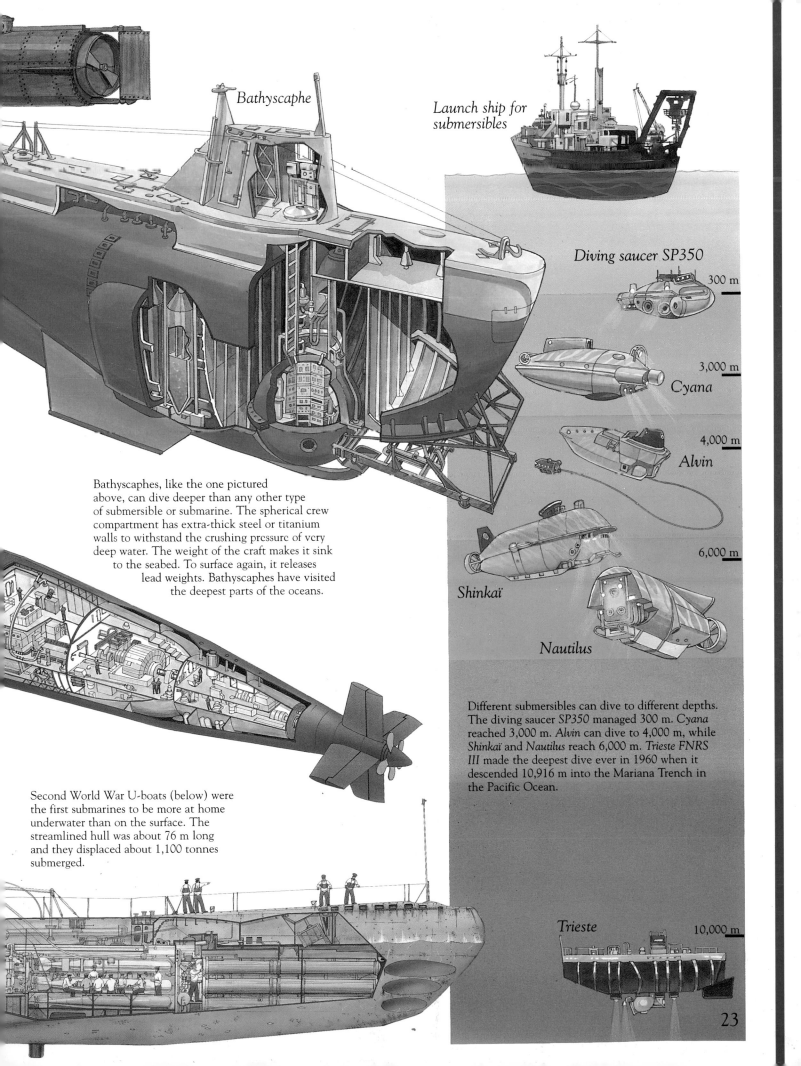

Bathyscaphe

Launch ship for submersibles

Diving saucer SP350

300 m

3,000 m

Cyana

4,000 m

Alvin

6,000 m

Shinkaï

Nautilus

Bathyscaphes, like the one pictured above, can dive deeper than any other type of submersible or submarine. The spherical crew compartment has extra-thick steel or titanium walls to withstand the crushing pressure of very deep water. The weight of the craft makes it sink to the seabed. To surface again, it releases lead weights. Bathyscaphes have visited the deepest parts of the oceans.

Different submersibles can dive to different depths. The diving saucer *SP350* managed 300 m. *Cyana* reached 3,000 m. *Alvin* can dive to 4,000 m, while *Shinkaï* and *Nautilus* reach 6,000 m. *Trieste FNRS III* made the deepest dive ever in 1960 when it descended 10,916 m into the Mariana Trench in the Pacific Ocean.

Second World War U-boats (below) were the first submarines to be more at home underwater than on the surface. The streamlined hull was about 76 m long and they displaced about 1,100 tonnes submerged.

Trieste

10,000 m

Floating Palaces

Oceangoing passenger liners are the most luxurious ships afloat and some resemble floating palaces. The golden age of the ocean liner was the first half of the 20th century. The great ships competed with each other to make the fastest passage across the North Atlantic. The fastest could make the crossing in less than a week. Their names became famous – the *Queen Mary*, *Normandie*, *Mauretania*, *Lusitania*, *United States* and *France*. They not only transported the wealthiest travellers but also carried thousands of poorer Europeans to new lives in America, Canada and Australia. However, the great liners could not compete with the arrival of jet airliners after the Second World War, and most of them have long since been scrapped.

In 1912, the largest and most luxurious liner of all was the RMS *Titanic*. It was thought to be unsinkable. On 10th April, it set sail from Southampton on its maiden voyage to New York with over 2,200 people on board. On the night of 14th April it struck an iceberg about 640 km south of Newfoundland and rapidly took in water. Three hours later, it sank beneath the icy water with the loss of more than 1,500 lives. On 1st September 1985, a team of American and French scientists discovered the *Titanic*'s last resting place 4,000 m down on the ocean floor. They glided over it in submersibles, filming and photographing every part of it. Since then, thousands of objects have been brought up from the wreck.

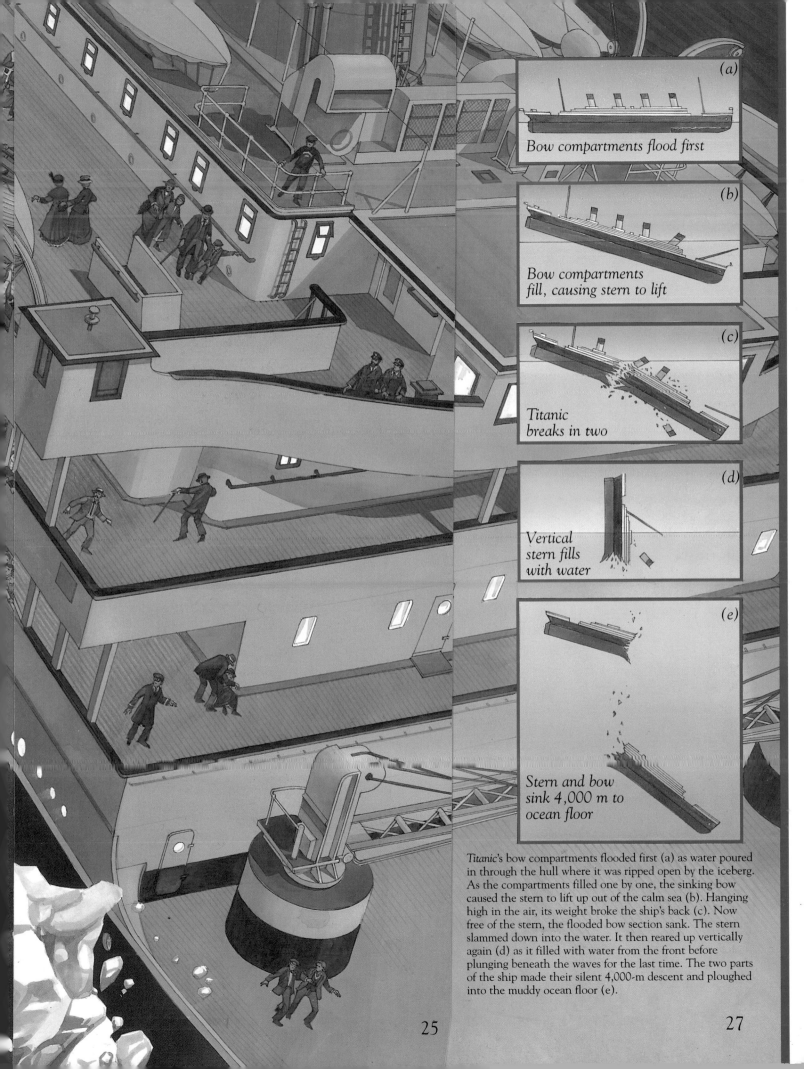

(a) Bow compartments flood first

(b) Bow compartments fill, causing stern to lift

(c) Titanic breaks in two

(d) Vertical stern fills with water

(e) Stern and bow sink 4,000 m to ocean floor

Titanic's bow compartments flooded first (a) as water poured in through the hull where it was ripped open by the iceberg. As the compartments filled one by one, the sinking bow caused the stern to lift up out of the calm sea (b). Hanging high in the air, its weight broke the ship's back (c). Now free of the stern, the flooded bow section sank. The stern slammed down into the water. It then reared up vertically again (d) as it filled with water from the front before plunging beneath the waves for the last time. The two parts of the ship made their silent 4,000-m descent and ploughed into the muddy ocean floor (e).

25

27

A gondola (below) is a type of boat found only in Venice. A gondolier standing at the stern steers and propels the boat by sweeping movements of one long oar.

Gondolier

Competitive rowing (left) is a popular sport. The boats are long and thin, and the rowers sit on sliding seats. In some races, a coxswain sits in the stern to steer the boat and calls out the timing for rowing.

Gondola

Oceangoing yachts (below) have competed for the prestigious America's Cup since 1851. The shape of the yachts, from their keels to their sails, are designed on computer and built using the latest materials for maximum speed.

Sailing for Fun

Boats are not just used for carrying passengers and cargo – people have fun with them, too. Families go sailing in pleasure yachts and cabin cruisers. The biggest sailing ships, called tall ships, are used for races and to train young sailors. There are races between powerboats, rowboats and all types of yachts, and even the Olympic Games include boat races. Some boat races are held on courses marked with buoys, while others take place between ports, around islands, across oceans, or even all the way around the world. Some races are for solo sailors while others are for teams. A famous boat race between teams of eight rowers from the universities of Oxford and Cambridge has been held on the River Thames in London almost every year since 1829.

La Gran Argentina

Daniel Scioli streaked through the waves toward the finish line to win his fourth world offshore powerboat championship in *La Gran Argentina* (above) in 1997. While Scioli piloted (steered) the long slender boat, Jorge Bordas controlled its throttle (engine speed).

Lifeboats are designed to stay afloat in the roughest seas so that they can rescue sailors, surfers and swimmers in distress. Most modern lifeboats are self-righting: if they capsize (turn over), they automatically roll upright again. Small inflatable rescue craft deal with emergencies close to shore, while larger boats handle rescues farther out to sea.

Spirit of Australia

In 1978, Ken Warby set the current official water speed record of 514 kph with his jet-powered hydroplane *Spirit of Australia*. He set the record on the Blowering Dam Lake in New South Wales, Australia.

RNLI (Royal National Lifeboat Institution) lifeboat

Life raft

It is essential to carry the right safety equipment at sea. Every boat must carry a first aid kit to deal with minor injuries. A horn, flares and a flashlight can attract attention in fog or at night. Larger oceangoing boats must carry a life raft.

Glossary

Aircraft carrier
A warship that has a runway on its deck for aircraft to land on and take off from.

Ballast tanks
Containers inside a submarine that can be flooded with sea water to make the submarine sink. When compressed air is blown into the tanks, the water is pushed out and the submarine rises again.

Bow
The front end of a boat or ship.

Catamaran
A boat with two hulls linked.

Coxswain
The person who sits at the stern of a racing rowboat, called a shell, and steers it. The coxswain also calls out the timing for the rowers to row.

Displacement
The weight of water replaced, or pushed aside, by the hull of a boat or ship sitting in the water.

Galley
A ship with rows of oarsmen.

Hull
The main body of a boat or ship from the deck downward.

Hydroplane
A small, fast powerboat designed to skim across the water's surface. Fins used to steer submarines are also called hydroplanes.

Keel
The part of a boat or ship that extends along the bottom of the hull from bow to stern.

Radar
Radio detection and ranging. A device for locating objects that are too far away to see by bouncing a burst of radio waves off them and measuring the time for the reflections to return.

Rigging
The ropes that hold a boat's masts and sails in position.

Sonar
Sound navigation and ranging. A device used by submarines for locating objects underwater by bouncing pulses of sound off them and measuring the time for the echoes to return. Also called echo location.

Spanish Armada
A fleet of warships sent by Philip II of Spain to attack England in 1588.

Stern
The back end of a boat or ship.

Submersible
A mini-submarine that is launched at sea and recovered again by a specially built mother-ship.

U-boat
A German submarine developed in the First World War and also used in the Second World War, from the German word *Unterseeboot*, meaning undersea boat.

Ships and Submarines Facts

For hundreds of years, sailors navigated at sea by observing the positions of the sun, moon and stars.

The left side of a ship (looking from stern to bow) is called port and the right side is starboard.

The speed of a ship at sea is measured in knots. One knot is equal to 1.852 kph.

The first large warship in the world with an iron hull was the British *HMS Warrior*, built in 1860.

The bathyscaphe *Trieste* took four hours and 48 minutes to descend 10,916 m into the Pacific Ocean in 1960.

Early steamships also had masts and sails in case their steam engines broke down.

When the liner *Titanic* sank in 1912 after striking an iceberg, the International Ice Patrol was established to warn ships of icebergs.

Some of the fastest military ships are powered by jet engines similar to those that power fighters and airliners.

Hydrofoils are boats that rise up out of the water as they speed up, supported by underwater wings.

A submarine at a depth of 100 m is totally unaffected by even the worst storm at the surface.

The depth of a ship's hull that is below the water is called its draught.

Russian Alfa class submarines are the fastest, with a top speed of about 80 kph. Their titanium hull enables them to dive to a depth of about 900 m.

The biggest cargo ship in the world is the *Jahre Viking*. It is 458 m long, 68 m wide and weighs 573,786 tonnes when fully loaded.

Ships and aeroplanes are said to have vanished in a part of the Atlantic Ocean called the Bermuda Triangle. The area is between Bermuda, Puerto Rico and Miami.

Chronology

4000 BC The date of the earliest known images of river boats, sailing boats and ships found as rock carvings and paintings on Egyptian pottery.

600 BC Pharaoh Necho II of Egypt sends a ship to explore the coast of Africa. It is the first known sea voyage around Africa.

AD 150 Arab sailors develop a new type of sail, the lateen sail, that enables boats to sail at an angle to the wind. Until then, boats could only sail in the same direction as the wind.

800 Longships carry the Vikings on raids along the coasts of northern Europe.

1000 Leif Eriksson sails to America and establishes a Viking settlement there.

1492 Christopher Columbus sets out on his first voyage of discovery to the New World.

1497 The Portuguese explorer Vasco da Gama sets sail to find a new route around Africa to India.

1588 The Spanish Armada is defeated by the English fleet.

1606 A Dutch sailor Willen Jantszoon is the first European to reach Australia.

1620 The first submarine is built by Dutchman Cornelis Drebbel.

1759 John Harrison invents a very accurate marine chronometer (clock) to enable a ship's position to be calculated more precisely.

1775 David Bushnell builds a one-man submarine called the *Turtle* to attack British ships during the American War of Independence.

1781 The Marquis de Jouffroy d'Abbans designs a steamboat called *Pyroscaphe*.

1819 The *Savannah*, a paddle steamer, is the first steamship to cross the Atlantic Ocean.

1843 Isambard Kingdom Brunel's ship, the *Great Britain*, is the first large ship to be built entirely of iron.

1845 The propeller-powered *Rattler* beat the *Alecto* in a tug of war to decide whether paddlewheels or propellers were best.

1851 The schooner *America* wins the annual Round the Isle of Wight race and is awarded a silver trophy that becomes known as America's Cup.

1869 The Suez Canal is completed, enabling ships to sail from the Mediterranean Sea to the Red Sea without sailing around Africa.

1875 The Plimsoll Line (or International Load Line) is introduced by Samuel Plimsoll. The line, painted on the side of a ship, ensures that it is not overloaded.

1897 The *Turbinia* is the first steamship to be propelled by a steam turbine.

1900 Irishman John Philip Holland builds the first successful modern submarine.

1910 An aircraft takes off from a ship for the first time, proving that aircraft carriers are possible.

1912 The passenger liner RMS *Titanic* sinks in the North Atlantic after striking an iceberg on her maiden voyage.

1943 Britain uses midget submarines to lay explosives under a German battleship.

1947 The explorer Thor Heyerdahl sails across the Pacific Ocean in a balsa-wood boat called *Kon-tiki* to prove that the Incas could have sailed from South America to the Pacific Islands.

1955 The US submarine *Nautilus*, the first nuclear-powered submarine, is launched.

1958 The *Nautilus* is the first submarine to reach the North Pole.

1959 The first hovercraft, designed by Sir Christopher Cockerell, makes its first 'flight'.

1960 The bathyscaphe *Trieste* sets a new deep-diving record of 10,916 m.

1968 The oceangoing passenger liner *Queen Elizabeth II* is launched.

1978 The oil tanker *Amoco Cadiz* runs aground on the French coast, spilling over 200,000 tonnes of oil.

1982 The remains of Henry VIII's ship the *Mary Rose*, which sank in 1545, are raised and preserved.

1983 America loses the America's Cup for the first time in the race's 132-year history. The Australian yacht *Australia II* is the winner.

1985 A team of American and French scientists discover the wreck of the liner *Titanic*.

1986 The *Wind Star*, a passenger liner with computer-controlled sails, is launched.

1989 The oil tanker *Exxon Valdiz* runs aground in Prince William Sound in the Gulf of Alaska and spills 41 million litres of oil.

1992 The Main-Danube Canal is completed, linking rivers to provide a continuous waterway from the North Sea to the Baltic Sea.

1995 America loses the America's Cup for only the second time in 144 years. The winner is the New Zealand yacht *Black Magic*.

1999 Victoria Murden, a lawyer from Kentucky in the USA, is the first woman to row across the Atlantic Ocean.

2001 A shipwreck is found off the coast of Panama. It could be the *Vizcaina*, one of the ships used by Christopher Columbus on his last voyage to the Americas in 1503.

Index